CAPITAL SPLENDOR

Gardens and Parks of Washington, DC

CAPITAL SPLENDOR

Gardens and Parks of Washington, DC

Text by Barbara Glickman
Photography by Valerie Brown

THE COUNTRYMAN PRESS
WOODSTOCK, VERMONT

Maps by Paul Woodward, © The Countryman Press
Book design and composition by Eugenie S. Delaney

Capital Splendor
978-0-88150-982-3

Published by The Countryman Press, P.O. Box 748,
Woodstock, VT 05091

Distributed by W. W. Norton & Company, Inc.,
500 Fifth Avenue, New York, NY 10110

Printed in China

10 9 8 7 6 5 4 3 2

This book is dedicated to my sons, Teddy and Sandy, who
visited these parks and gardens numerous times, as well as many
others throughout the world. Their love of exploring natural areas
or formal manicured gardens has been a pleasure to behold.
BARBARA GLICKMAN

I dedicate this book to my parents, Connie and Marvin Brown,
for their support and encouragement and for showing me
the value of hard work in the pursuit of one's passions.
VALERIE BROWN

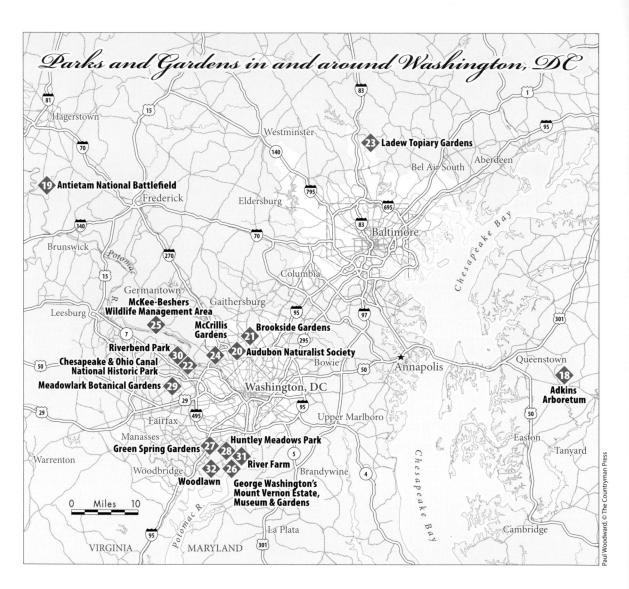

Parks and Gardens in and around Washington, DC

23 Ladew Topiary Gardens

19 Antietam National Battlefield

McKee-Beshers
Wildlife Management Area

25

McCrillis
Gardens

Brookside Gardens

21

Riverbend Park

30 **24** **20** Audubon Naturalist Society

Chesapeake & Ohio Canal
National Historic Park

22

Meadowlark Botanical Gardens **29**

18

Adkins
Arboretum

Washington, DC

Green Spring Gardens **27** Huntley Meadows Park

28 **31** River Farm

32 **26**

Woodlawn

George Washington's
Mount Vernon Estate,
Museum & Gardens

VIRGINIA   MARYLAND

Paul Woodward, © The Countryman Press

Hagerstown
Westminster
Bel Air South   Aberdeen
Frederick   Eldersburg   Baltimore   Chesapeake Bay
Brunswick
Germantown   Gaithersburg
Leesburg   Columbia
Queenstown
Fairfax   Bowie
Manasses
Warrenton   Woodbridge
Brandywine   Chesapeake Bay   Easton   Tanyard
La Plata   Cambridge

0   Miles   10

Potomac R.

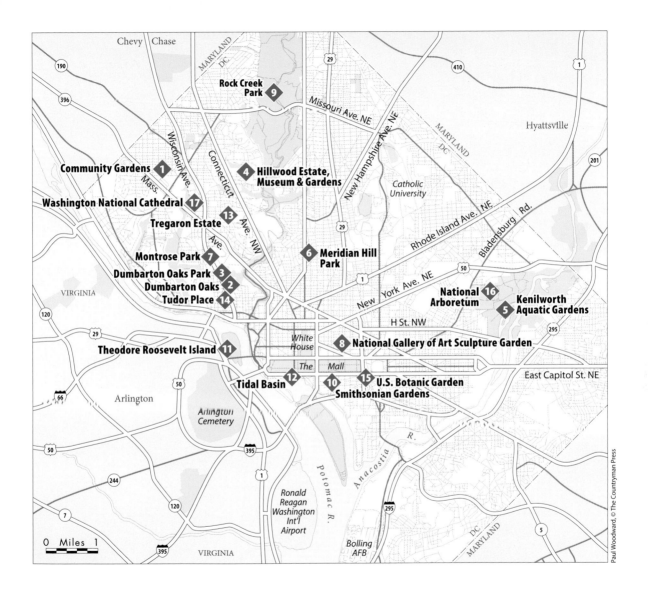

Community Gardens 1

Hillwood Estate, Museum & Gardens 4

Rock Creek Park 9

Washington National Cathedral 17

Tregaron Estate 13

Montrose Park 7

Meridian Hill Park 6

Dumbarton Oaks Park 3

Dumbarton Oaks 2

Tudor Place 14

National Arboretum 16

Kenilworth Aquatic Gardens 5

Theodore Roosevelt Island 11

National Gallery of Art Sculpture Garden 8

Tidal Basin 12

U.S. Botanic Garden 15

Smithsonian Gardens 10

Paul Woodward, © The Countryman Press

Contents

Acknowledgments   10

Foreword   12

Introduction   14

I. DISTRICT OF COLUMBIA

Acknowledgments

W E OWE THANKS to our publisher, The Countryman Press, for supporting our idea for this book and putting it into print, especially to editors Kermit Hummel, Caitlin Martin, and Lisa Sacks.

We are grateful to the many garden directors and their staffs, historic home directors, and park superintendents who gave permission to take photographs to be used in the book. We also want to thank them for their help in identifying some of the plants and butterflies.

We especially want to thank Gail Griffin, Executive Director of Dumbarton Oaks, and Holly Shimizu, Executive Director of the United States Botanic Garden, who provided initial support for our project. We are highly indebted to you, for we feel our project might not have gone forward without your support.

We also offer our thanks to Lynn Rossotti, Bill Johnson, and Lauren Chapan Salazar, Hillwood Estate, Museum & Gardens; Bonnie LePard, Tregaron Estate; Mandy Katz and Suzanne Bouchard, Tudor Place; Beth Schnakenberg, Kyle Wallick, and Barbara Faust, the United States Botanic Garden; Dr. Ramon Jordan, the United States National Arboretum; Richard Weinberg and Toni Kislear, Washington National Cathedral; Ellie Altman, Adkins Arboretum; Leslie McDermott, Brookside Gardens; Barbara Barnoff,

Ladew Topiary Gardens; Melissa Wood, Dean Norton, and Peggy Bowers, George Washington's Mount Vernon Estate, Museum & Gardens; Sandy Rittenhouse-Black, Green Spring Gardens; Keith Tomlinson and Tammy Burke, Meadowlark Botanical Gardens; David Ellis and Sue Galvin, River Farm; Laurie Ossman, Woodlawn; Emily Schneider, Bread for the City; Jeff Kleinman, Folio Literary Management, LLC; Alexandra Gray, intern; Betsy Berlin for technical support and graphic design; Dale Gurvis Photography; Marvin Brown for photo and text consulting; Gary Glickman for technical support; Mark and Marianne Mandell Brown; Diana Morgan; Jim van Sweden for instilling a love of garden photography; and others we may have overlooked.

Purple tulips border the curvilinear brick path at the Smithsonian Gardens' Mary Livingston Ripley Garden.

Foreword

GARDENS IN THE WASHINGTON, DC, area have come a long way in the last 30 years—with great improvements in their quality. With this evolution our parks and gardens have expanded, developed, and grown along with the horticulturists who care for them. Take Dumbarton Oaks, for example, where under the guidance of Gail Griffin, the gardens have regained much of their original splendor. Another great example are the Smithsonian Gardens that have blossomed with the care and guidance of amazing horticulturists; the gardens have become outdoor, living museums for the millions of visitors to Washington, DC. Our gardens are more than simply the ornament around a building. Recognition that plants are essential to human lives for health, as well as for the health of our ecosystem, provides added motivation for planting appropriately and sensitively. While art and great design are fabulous and excit-ing, so are the variety of birds you can attract to your garden, or the kinds of butterflies and other pollinators that will come with the right plantings. Our enhanced understanding of the importance of plants is evidenced in our gardens, providing inspiration as well as opportunities for learning and discovery. The gardens are a welcome respite from the stresses of daily life. Each tells stories of history, people, nature, places, cultures, experiences, journeys, and ceremonies. Their complexities are reflected in this book, *Capital Splendor: Gardens and Parks of Washington, DC.* Extraordinary photographs capture the light, seasons, textures, designs, and personalities of these phenomenal and varied outdoor spaces. There is no other current book that so completely gathers and documents the best of this region's gardens. Whether used as an armchair visit to these wonderful places or as the source of

documented beauty for each particular place, this book will find a useful spot in our homes and libraries.

Holly H. Shimizu
EXECUTIVE DIRECTOR
US BOTANIC GARDEN
December 7, 2010

ABOVE: *An enchanting trompe l'oeil screen at the eastern border of Dumbarton Oaks depicts a fountain in a niche, leaving the visitor to wonder what lies beyond.*

Introduction

PEOPLE THE WORLD OVER share a passion for gardens and parks. Residents and tourists visit the well-known sights the Washington region has to offer, but many remain unaware of the glorious beauty that awaits in the gardens and parks that enrich the area. Washington is unique in the diversity of them, which range from formal manicured landscapes to extraordinary topiary gardens to spectacular waterfalls and gorges to freshwater wetlands. The photographs and descriptions in *Capital Splendor: Gardens and Parks of Washington, DC* showcase the wealth of gardens and parks in the Washington, DC, region.

Gardens provide stimulation to all the senses, yet are among the most relaxing places in the world. Think of touching the velvety softness of a lamb's ear plant, or inhaling the heady aroma of a rose, or tasting the fresh basil and tomatoes of summer, or hearing the cattails swaying with the slightest of breezes, or seeing thousands of sunflowers in a field. All these senses will be stirred as you examine the photographs.

A visit to a garden or park requires a certain amount of receptiveness, physically, mentally, and sensorially. These places invite one to walk, hike, or even scramble while using all the senses to absorb the natural wonders. The sensory challenge allows you to slow down and marvel at details you might not normally take note of, to become engrossed.

The national, state, and regional parks described within possess an abundance of flora, fauna, and natural marvels. The gardens, ponds, meadows, forests, and boulders are home to fish, insects, amphibians, mammals, and birds. Take the time to look for some of the shy or quick darting ones, such as the five-lined skink you might find in a dead tree trunk in the woods or on the rocks.

Numerous Vanda cultivar orchids are on display in the Conservatory in the United States Botanic Garden.

The narrative for each park or garden includes a brief history as well as an overview and the site's outstanding or unique features. The 32 gardens or parks portrayed are all within an hour and a half drive from Washington, DC. Many offer stunning or unique garden or geological features. More than 10 of them are associated with historic mansions, some of which are available for touring. If you take the tour, or just read about the inspired individuals who had the imagination to build their homes and gardens, you will be amply rewarded. Site information, including the garden or park's address, phone number, and website, is provided at the back of the book. Many gardens post the average bloom times on their websites.

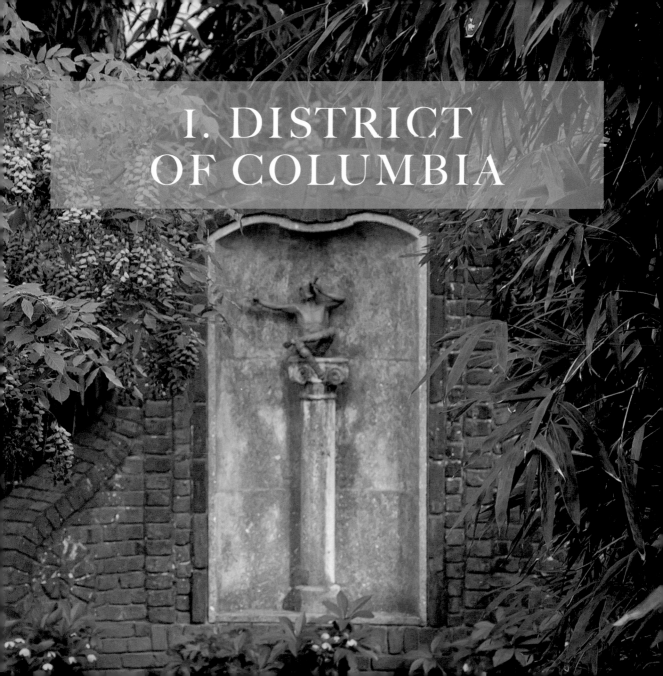

I. DISTRICT OF COLUMBIA

1.
Community Gardens of Washington, DC

W ASHINGTON, DC, has approximately 40 community gardens spread throughout the city's wards. Some are in very urban settings, such as Independence Community Garden opposite the National Air and Space Museum, while the pastoral Rock Creek Community Garden looks onto a horse paddock surrounded by forest.

Many of the country's community gardens arose at the end of the 19th century, when cities grew quickly and poor residents were offered garden plots on which to grow food. During World War I and World War II, victory gardens became morale boosters, since the populace felt good about their contribution to the war effort. In addition to those original purposes, community gardens today serve additional roles, such as providing a meeting place for people of many backgrounds, providing a peaceful, nurturing site, and sometimes in otherwise uninviting parts of a city, affording a place in which to grow chemical-free food, or simply allowing people to grow their own food. Rooftop gardens are becoming

ABOVE: *Bread for the City's rooftop garden makes use of all its space; clay pots along the wall hold geraniums.*

LEFT: *At the Newark Street Community Garden, people grow flowers, such as roses, in addition to edible plants.*

popular, and Bread for the City, an agency that provides food and other services to the city's poor, has the first large-scale agricultural project in the city. Its large rooftop vegetable garden provides food for its pantries and cooking workshops.

The website www.fieldtoforknetwork .org has comprehensive and useful information on the different community gardens, including contact person, amenities of each site, plot size, and waiting list.

ABOVE: *Peppers, daisies, lettuce, and tomatoes are just a sample of the plants grown at the Rock Creek Community Garden.*

LEFT: *Bell peppers ripen at the Newark Street Community Garden, near the Washington National Cathedral.*

2.

Dumbarton Oaks

THE VISUAL SPLENDOR of nature and magnificent landscape design awaits you at the formal gardens of Dumbarton Oaks, located in the lovely historic neighborhood of Georgetown. Mildred and Robert Woods Bliss purchased the original 53-acre property as their residence in 1920. In 1940, the house and gardens were given to Harvard University to serve as a research institute and museum to showcase their Byzantine and pre-Columbian art collection. The gardens today comprise 10 acres that surround the Bliss mansion. Outside the gardens, 27 acres form the Dumbarton Oaks Park, consisting of woodland, streams, and meadows. The park is owned by the U.S. government and administered by the U.S. Park Service.

Mildred Bliss started working with the

One of more than 50 benches, this lovely stone bench is in the eastern end of the Rose Garden. Stone leaves cascade over two shields above the Bliss motto, Quod Severis Metes (As you sow so shall you reap), carved into the bench.

landscape designer Beatrix Farrand in 1921. They collaborated for nearly 30 years on the garden design. Farrand had toured European gardens extensively and you can see Italian-, French-, and English-style garden influences. Throughout the garden are exquisite urns, balustrades, garden seats, gates, finials, steps, and stonework. Dumbarton Oaks, the culmination of Farrand's lifework, is considered by many to be one of the finest gardens in the United States.

Terraces divide the hilly landscape into various garden rooms, each one nearly hidden from the next. Walls created by trees, hedges, and gates further define the

A pavilion in one of the three Kitchen Gardens designed by Beatrix Farrand
with a bell-shaped terra-cotta-tile roof belies its function as a tool shed.

Wisteria is at its peak in the Arbor Terrace.

rooms. Gardens closer to the house are more formal in design than those down the sloping terrain. Each room is a unique garden offering its own special sensory delights. Three paths traverse the upper and lower parts of the garden, offering spectacular views, opportunities for exploration, and delicious surprises. Approximately 50 benches, most also designed by Beatrix Farrand, invite the visitor to sit and reflect.

The gardens were designed so that they would be a delight for all seasons. Borders burst with color as spring bulbs bloom, followed by perennials as spring turns to summer. Chrysanthemums take over in autumn, and in winter there are blooming perennials and evergreens. The exquisite blend of color, texture, shape, and form evolves throughout the year. One of the best garden rooms in which to experience the wonderful array of seasonal color is the Herbaceous Border.

Upon entering Dumbarton Oaks, one is greeted by a large katsura tree with heavy horizontal branches that reach across the sprawling lawn. Follow the shaded path where a statue of Pan directs you to Lovers' Lane Pool, a shallow oval pool overlooked by a small Roman-style amphitheater with terraced brick rows. You can sit and admire the columns, vine-covered lattice, reflections in the water, and vistas down the hills and beyond to the woodland on the other side of the park valley. Stroll along the Prunus Walk, the middle path going north and south, to explore the three Kitchen Gardens that

An 18th-century Provencal fountain amidst an aquatic garden is located in the center of the Ellipse, where a double row of American hornbeams frames the garden's perimeter. The Ellipse is one of the most peaceful areas of the garden.

are as decorative as they are utilitarian. The high brick walls soak up the sun's warmth and in turn support fruit trees.

The Rose Garden was a favorite of the Blisses, and it houses a crypt containing their ashes. Roses bloom in the spring, summer, and autumn, presenting a nearly continuous show of fragrant blooms from May through October. Rose bushes are set in a geometric pattern with boxwood providing the green background in summer and color in winter. Two iron balconies at one end overlook the Fountain Terrace, a garden of timeless grace featuring seasonal flowers and two fountains, each one with a putto holding a fish. The Urn Terrace, the prelude to the Rose Garden, is stunningly beautiful and fragrant; wisteria and jasmine adorn the wall overlooking the roses. Wisteria-covered walls add to the luxuriant grandeur of the view to the large Pebble Garden, the site of a former tennis court. Nearby are the Horseshoe Steps, an elegant curved staircase and fountain leading to the breathtaking swimming pool. Lastly, the Orangery, with its large creeping fig and tropical plants, makes for a lovely respite on a cold winter's day.

ABOVE: *Mexican pebbles create a mosaic with a wheat sheaf motif in the Pebble Garden, enclosed by wisteria-covered walls. The beds are filled with thyme and sedum.*

LEFT: *Cherry trees show their autumn colors.*

3

Dumbarton Oaks Park

DUMBARTON OAKS PARK comprises 27 acres on the northern border of Dumbarton Oaks garden and is part of the original estate bought by Mildred and Robert Bliss. It was given to the National Park Service in 1940. The entrance to the park is via a gate down Lovers' Lane at R Street, NW, east of the garden.

The park appears to be a wilderness waiting to be explored, compared to the adjacent well-tended garden. Beatrix Farrand designed these acres as well as those at Dumbarton Oaks, and her intent was to make the land natural and countrified. Steps near the stream trail go up to an old stone gated doorway separating the garden and park. Overgrown meadows, woodland, moss-covered benches, waterfalls, bridges, and trails make for a very bucolic

ABOVE: *This is one of many stone bridges that cross the brook.*

LEFT: *A gate separates the beautiful gardens of Dumbarton Oaks from the more natural landscape of Dumbarton Oaks Park.*

setting. Several stone footbridges allow access to the stream trail or the upland trail overlooking the meadow. Benches are scattered throughout, even in the midst of the meadow's tallest grasses. When you are near the dammed waterhole and see the abundant greenery of the nearby rhododendrons and hear the soothing sound of small waterfalls, you almost have the illusion of being in a tropical setting. Invasive vines have overtaken parts of the park; however, there are plans to restore the park to its former state.

4.

Hillwood Estate, Museum & Gardens

HILLWOOD ESTATE, MUSEUM & GARDENS are the former home of Marjorie Merriweather Post. They include a marvelous collection of formal garden rooms, lawns, and woods. The gardens of Hillwood are located adjacent to Rock Creek Park in northwest Washington, DC.

Marjorie Merriweather Post inherited the Post cereal company in 1914, and in 1955 bought Hillwood, after her divorce from her third husband, Joseph Davies, the second United States ambassador to Russia. She renovated the 1920s estate inside and out from 1955 to 1957 and envisioned the home as a future museum to house her collection of Imperial Russian and 18th- and 19th-century French decorative arts. Mrs. Post redesigned formal garden rooms out of the landscape to showcase mature specimens outside, just as she showcased her collection of Russian Orthodox Church objects inside the mansion. It was known that Mrs. Post thought nothing of moving a 75-foot, 18.5-ton elm tree to enhance a view!

Mrs. Post's favorite area was the Lunar Lawn, an idyllic

A stone pathway and bridge skirt the pool in the Japanese-style garden.

and other trees and shrubs surround the lawn. Today, you can sit on one of the many original chairs and see the Washington Monument 6 miles away.

Just beyond the lawn, the satyr musicians beckon you to the Japanese-style garden, a replica of the mountainous landscape of Japan. As you walk across stone walking trails and bridges, notice the waterfalls, pools, sculpture, rocks, Japanese and native plants, and fish.

The French Parterre is a wonderful garden just outside the mansion's drawing room. In keeping with its design, which is a typical formal 18th-century French garden, four quadrants of boxwood surround gravel footpaths that encircle a small pool with putti sculptures spouting water. Be sure to sit awhile and take in the statue of Diana, goddess of nature, at the far end, and marble sphinxes on the balustrade.

Beyond the French Parterre is the Rose Garden, whose tulips and wisteria bestow color and a heady scent before the roses take center stage. Wisteria and climbing roses grace the brick and wood pergola. Mrs. Post enhanced the original rose garden by adding boxwood and the brick

backdrop for hosting social events. It is a large crescent-shaped lawn whose borders are always blooming with colorful spring tulips, summer annuals, or autumn chrysanthemums. Camellias, azaleas, elms,

path, and she designed the rose garden so that each bed had a unique floribunda rose.

Other garden areas to explore include the Four Seasons Overlook with its four statues, each representing one of the seasons; the Putting Green with its clipped turf and viburnum and other fragrant plants and trees; the Friendship Walk, a walkway with rhododendrons and azaleas; the Pet Cemetery, filled with canine statuary to honor Mrs. Post's pet dogs; the Motor Court, with its statue of Eros and tall dawn redwoods; and the Greenhouse with its many orchids and tropical plants.

Diana, the Roman goddess of the hunt, beckons you to linger in the French parterre with its English ivy walls and playful putti.

ABOVE: *The Four Seasons Overlook has statues symbolizing the seasons.*

LEFT: *Spring tulips and azaleas provide a colorful border to the Lunar Lawn.*

Azaleas frame the Friendship Walk, with a view of Mrs. Post's house in the background.

Mrs. Post's ashes are in the base of a pink granite monument in the center of the Rose Garden.

5.

Kenilworth Aquatic Gardens

OCATED IN THE NORTHEASTERN corner of Washington, DC, near the Maryland border, Kenilworth Aquatic Gardens is the only national park dedicated to the cultivation and presentation of water plants. A network of 44 artificial ponds of different sizes and shapes comprises a natural environment endowed with a variety of species of birds, insects, mammals, amphibians, and plants. But the real jewels are the plants that thrive in the water, the Aquatic Gardens.

The gardens were started in 1880 by Mr. Walter Shaw, who purchased 37 acres of marshland along the Anacostia River. What started as a hobby, growing hardy American water lilies in an ice pond, became a thriving business, W. B. Shaw Lily Ponds. He and his daughter developed new lilies, including the Pink Opal and the W. B. Shaw, and sold these and others that they imported from around the world. Thousands of people, including dignitaries such as President Coolidge and President

A heron patrols the grounds.

Wilson, walked the grounds when the gardens were opened to the general public on Sunday mornings. In 1938 the property was sold to the National Park Service and given the name Kenilworth, after a local community.

Grassy paths serve as dikes separating the ponds that cover 12 acres, and the water level in the ponds is controlled by a system of underground pipes. Adjacent to the gardens is the 77-acre Kenilworth Marsh, a tidal wetland. An aboveground boardwalk with two observation platforms goes from the ponds to the Kenilworth Marsh. Starting near the Visitor Center, you can also take the River Trail that borders a wooded swamp and tidal marsh and reaches the Anacostia River after nearly ¾ mile.

The garden's aquatic plants include water lilies, lotuses, and cattail. The lilies are at their peak in early to mid-summer; the best time to observe them is in the early morning as they close when the day gets hot. The hardy lilies peak from mid-June to mid-July. Tropical lilies peak in July and August, and include the large Amazon water lily with its fragrant nocturnal blooms. These giant lily pads grow to 6 feet in diameter and make wonderful homes for the populous frogs. The lotuses also peak in late July through August and can grow to be 6 feet high.

Perhaps equally enthralling, especially for younger visitors, is the large variety of creatures that make the gardens their home, such as beavers, fox, deer, frogs, salamanders, skinks, turtles, non-poisonous snakes, and fish. It is always a thrill to walk the boardwalk and see herons in the mud flats, and you may see other birds, such as osprey, sparrows, and bald eagles. You are also likely to see such insects as butterflies, water boatmen beetles, and dragonflies;

The white-flowered 'Missouri' water lily, a tropical night bloomer, is lovely and fragrant.

mosquitoes are a tasty treat for the many predators who keep them under control. A Water Lily Festival is held the fourth Saturday in July, and park rangers give tours on summer weekends.

The inverted-cone-shaped seed pod of a lotus plant resembles a showerhead.

Dirt or grassy paths with benches circle the many ponds.

6.

Meridian Hill Park

MERIDIAN HILL PARK occupies 12 acres in northwest Washington, DC. It has as its borders 15th, 16th, W, and Euclid streets NW. The park's classical Italian landscape design is probably the most impressive of any in this country, and it is what makes this park unique and a must-see. If you like order, symmetry, fountains, and statues in your garden, you will be delighted by its stunning beauty.

The park's name derives from a mansion built here in the early 1800s that was sited on the exact longitude of the city's original milestone marker on 16th Street. The marker was used by Pierre Charles L'Enfant, the French architect and engineer known for designing the layout of Washington, DC's streets on a north-south axis. The park's history is varied, having once served as the location of the precursor to George Washington University and as an encampment for Union troops. In 1914 the landscape architect George Burnap was hired by the Department of Interior to design a formal park similar to Italian gardens found in the great cities of the world. The park opened in 1936, was designated a National Historic Landmark for its neoclassical design in 1994, and is administered by Rock Creek Park.

Meridian Hill Park appears to be a Renaissance villa landscape with its 13 cascading water basins, reflecting pools, tiered gardens, symmetrical staircases, and

The elegant park is near many vibrant city neighborhoods.

The reflecting pool exhibits the park's majesty.

abundant statuary and urns. There is a lower and an upper part to the park. The upper flat part has long grassy fields and a wonderful terrace overlooking the lower part, affording a great view of the city. The reflecting pool at the lowest southern end has water lilies in the summer and is bordered by a large plaza. The construction medium of concrete aggregate was first used at Meridian Hill Park for its walls, balustrades, planting containers, etc. Small pebbles of a certain size and color were chosen for the architectural shapes and then the texture was revealed through wire brushing and acid washing. The park was neglected for several years, but it is once again vibrant and attracts an ever more diverse group of people reflective of the city's growth. The Sunday drum circle has been a popular tradition for many decades.

ABOVE: *Italian garden concepts add to the grandeur of the cascading waterfall.*

LEFT: *Dogwood and redbud trees frame the reflecting pool.*

7.

Montrose Park

MONTROSE PARK occupies 16 acres in
Georgetown between Dumbarton
Oaks Park and Oak Hill Cemetery.
It is part of Rock Creek Park and managed
by the National Park Service.

Robert Parrott, a 19th-century industrial-
ist, bought the property sometime between
1804 and 1813 to make rope. The lovely
brick walkway stretching from R Street to the
playground was used for the purpose of lay-
ing out rope to be used in sailing ships. Parrott was known to allow the public to use the
land for picnics and meetings. After his death
in 1882, the property fell into decline and
was named Montrose Estate.

Sarah Louisa Rittenhouse, a Georgetown
resident, succeeded in getting Congress in
1910 to buy the acreage to establish the park.
George Burnap designed the park that is used
by families and dogs alike. As you gaze at the

The Georgetown neighborhood can be seen just beyond the rose garden near the park's entrance.

lovely shaded gazebo that overlooks one of the two sets of tennis courts surrounded by trees, you are reminded of earlier times. The gas lamp-lit walkway gives off a gentle glow in the evening.

The park also has a boxwood maze near the playground, a large, gently sloping lawn with oak and tulip trees, woodland, and benches overlooking Rock Creek Park.

Roses, lamb's ear plants, and a plaque honoring the creator of the park, Sarah Louisa Rittenhouse, are in the lovely garden at the entrance of the park.

8.
The National Gallery of Art Sculpture Garden

T HE NATIONAL GALLERY OF ART SCULPTURE Garden, occupying 6 acres adjacent to the gallery's West Building, exhibits magnificent art and plantings. The garden is bounded by Constitution Avenue NW, Madison Drive NW, 7th Street NW, and 9th Street NW. Seventeen works of sculpture from the gallery are displayed throughout the garden. The plantings, maintained by the National Gallery of Art horticulture staff, include canopy trees, shrubs, perennials, and ground covers.

The large fountain in the center of the garden puts on a wonderful water show when the jets of water spray to opposite sides of the fountain. The effect is more magical on a summer evening when the sun's rays paint the façade of the National Archives golden. Containers of tropical hibiscus are spaced around the fountain. Jazz concerts are held on Friday evenings in summer, and the fountain serves as an ice rink in winter. A double row of yews borders the fountain and white crape myrtles line the walkway near the fountain. Many of the borders are filled with liriope, and other borders are filled with cherry laurel and oak leaf hydrangea. Near the mall entrance, note the tall Kentucky coffee tree whose thick fruit pods contain large seeds or beans.

Cubi XI was one of 28 geometric steel shapes made by David Smith between 1961 and 1965.

Thinker on a Rock, *made of cast bronze, was completed by Barry Flanagan in 1997.*

The captivating jet sprays of the fountain are enhanced by the beauty of the National Archives in the background.

Typewriter Eraser, Scale X, *was completed by Claes Oldenburg and Coosje van Bruggen in 1999.*

9.

Rock Creek Park

R OCK CREEK PARK is an area of urban wilderness in Washington, DC, with approximately 1,750 acres, administered by the National Park Service. It extends from the Washington, DC, border with Montgomery County, Maryland, in the north to the Potomac River in the south. The approximately 4,000 adjoining acres in Maryland are called Rock Creek Regional Park and are administered by the Maryland-National Capital Park and Planning Commission.

The park was established by Congress in 1890 and is the oldest and one of the largest urban parks in the country. Frederick Law Olmsted, one of the nation's most famous park and city planners, advocated for the park's development for the benefit of all people. Many presidents hiked in the park; President Lincoln went to observe

Bikers take over the roads when closed to vehicular traffic.

the only Confederate assault on Washington, DC, during the Civil War from Fort Stevens, one of four Civil War fortifications in the park. It is said that President Lincoln came under direct fire during one of these visits. Walking around Fort Stevens, you can see the remnants of the trenches, cannon emplacements, and battlements.

Today the park includes a wide variety of recreational facilities in addition to an extensive system of walking and horse trails. These facilities include the only planetarium in the national park system, located at the Rock Creek Nature Center; Peirce Mills, a gristmill that was used for grinding wheat and corn into flour; the Carter Barron outdoor amphitheater; an 18-hole golf course; a tennis stadium; a zoo; playgrounds; and numerous group and public picnic areas. But for many people the park is just a wonderful retreat within the city. You would not think that neighborhoods adjoin this wooded wilderness. The natural and wild beauty of the park is apparent if you walk along the Rock Creek River Valley and look up into the woodland scenery. Although meadows abound, most of the park is covered by woodland that includes trees such as mountain laurel, pine, and tulip poplar. There are also deer, foxes, raccoons, and many types of birds and fish.

Dogs enjoy a good park outing.

ABOVE: *This small log cabin, now located on Beach Drive north of Military Road, belonged to the poet Joaquin Miller and was moved in 1912 from its location in Meridian Hill Park.*

LEFT: *Rock Creek Park is aptly named.*

ABOVE: *The reflection of trees and their roots in the stream looks like a spider web.*

LEFT: *Trees glisten in the fresh snow.*

The Smithsonian Gardens

MANY OF THE MUSEUMS of the Smithsonian Institution have outdoor gardens that are designed to complement and enhance their accompanying museums. Established in 1972, Smithsonian Gardens manages the gardens and indoor horticulture displays. Its mission is "to enrich the Smithsonian experience through exceptional gardens, horticulture exhibits, collections, and education." Although there are additional gardens, we will limit our descriptions to the following five: Enid A. Haupt Garden, Mary Livingston Ripley Garden, Katherine Dulin Folger Rose Garden, Butterfly Habitat Garden at the National Museum of Natural History, and the Victory Garden at the National Museum of American History, Behring Center.

Opened in 1987 and funded by Enid Annenburg Haupt, the 4.2-acre Enid A. Haupt Garden is located between Independence Avenue SW and the Smithsonian Castle. It is actually a rooftop garden above the Arthur M. Sackler Gallery, the National

The Kathrine Dulin Folger Rose Garden is nestled between the Smithsonian Castle and the Arts and Industries Building.

Museum of African Art, and the S. Dillon Ripley Center. There are three distinct gardens that mirror the museums' artistic traditions and architecture.

The parterre in the main garden has colorful plantings designed in symmetrical patterns. Every few years, the rectangular lawn is redesigned with motifs including fleurs-de-lis, scallops, or diamonds. And there are seasonal plantings, from the beautifully colorful array of pansies in the winter and spring to ornamental cabbages and kales in the autumn. Large saucer magnolias line the brick walkway. The parterre was a key element of Victorian design, and its use here complements the Smithsonian Castle's opulent architecture.

The Moongate Garden is next to the Arthur M. Sackler Gallery and Freer Gallery of Art. The Temple of Heaven in Beijing, China, influenced the garden's design, which has circles within squares representing heaven and earth. There are two 9-foot-high pink granite moon gates on opposing sides of the enclosed pool. Boxwood and dwarf mondo grass provide the greenery, and, in springtime, azaleas and magnolias add extra color.

Located next to the National Museum of African Art, the Fountain Garden was inspired by the Court of the Lions at Alhambra, the 13th-century Moorish palace in Granada, Spain. Islamic garden influences include its geometric symmetry, central fountain, and water channels. Water from a single jet shoots 8 feet in the air, offering a cool treat on a hot summer day, and there are water channels atop the low walls near the fountain.

The Mary Livingston Ripley Garden is located between the Arts and Industries Building and the Hirshhorn Museum and Sculpture Garden, and between Independence Avenue SW and the National Mall. It was named after Mrs. S. Dillon Ripley, wife of the eighth Secretary of the Smithsonian Institution, and an avid gardener and plant collector. She championed the idea of fully accessible raised planting beds so that everyone could touch and smell

Tulips border the entrance to the Mary Livingston Ripley Garden.

The meandering path winds through diverse butterfly habitats.

the plants. The garden is packed with delightful and whimsical treasures, from the 19th-century antique acanthus cast-iron fountain to the colorful birdhouses. Its curvilinear pathways summon you to enjoy the shaded secret garden and sit on one of the lovely cast-iron benches and be captivated by the profusion of trees, shrubs, annuals, perennials, hanging baskets, and some unusual plants. Be sure to see the high-climbing vine called a Dutchman's Pipe, a tropical with large seedpods, near the fountain and between the lampposts.

Also look for the Naranjillo plant, which has thorns protruding from the tops and bottoms of its very large leaves.

The Katherine Dulin Folger Rose Garden is in front of the Arts and Industries Building, just east of the Smithsonian Castle. A generous gift from Mr. and Mrs. Lee M. Folger and the Folger Fund created the garden. From mid-May through November, roses take center stage, with other annuals, perennials, and tropical plants providing color. Deciduous hollies and evergreen shrubs dominate in the wintertime.

Victorian benches in the Mary Livingston Ripley Garden's many alcoves provide a shady break.

The Butterfly Habitat Garden at the National Museum of Natural History is located between Constitution Avenue NW and the National Mall on the museum's east side. The garden's objective is to emphasize the partnerships between plants and butterflies. The four habitats that butterflies visit (wetland, meadow, wood's edge, and urban) are represented with many examples of plants. For example, monarch butterflies are attracted to many herbs, such as rosemary and mint, found in an urban garden. The garden is well labeled, showing the specific life cycle of a butterfly and its matching plant. Nectar plants support the adult butterfly and host plants support the earlier stages, and an example is shown of the black swallowtail caterpillar feeding on the leaves of Queen Anne's Lace plants.

The Victory Garden at the National Museum of American History, Behring Center, is located on the terrace outside the museum's cafeteria. It is a replica of a typical World War II-era vegetable garden that provided homegrown food to aid in the war effort. Over 50 types of vegetables are grown in the 130-foot-long garden.

Magnolia blossoms frame the Moon Gate and cherry tree blossoms embrace it.

The water attracts birds, and children often splash in the fountain.

11.

Theodore Roosevelt Island

THEODORE ROOSEVELT ISLAND, located in the
Potomac River between Washington, DC, and
Virginia and connected to the latter by a footbridge, is approximately 88.5 acres, .5 mile long, and
.25 mile wide. Many animals and birds, including deer,
foxes, rabbits, turtles, and blue herons, make their
home on the island.

The land has a long and varied history, having first
served as a seasonal fishing village for Native Americans.
One of the country's Founding Fathers, George Mason,
later owned it, and during the Civil War the Union
Army used it as a drill field. In 1931 the Theodore
Roosevelt Memorial Association purchased the island to
create a memorial to honor the president's commit-
ment to the conservation of public lands for national
parks, forests, and wildlife refuges. Frederick Law Olmsted Jr. designed the landscape by replacing the non-
native plants with 20,000 native hardwood shrubs and
trees; this was a public works project of the Civilian
Conservation Corps during the Great Depression. The

National Park Service maintains the park.

Two and one half miles of trails navigate upland forest, swamp, and tidal marsh. Much of the Swamp Trail is a boardwalk traversing the freshwater tidal marsh with its cattails and cypress trees. If you venture off the path at the northwestern end, you can catch glimpses of the sandy beach or Georgetown. Closer to the western end is the Memorial Plaza, which includes a large bronze statue of Theodore Roosevelt, two large fountains, and a moat.

The boardwalk on the island's east side passes over marshes and swamp.

Many deer make their home on Theodore Roosevelt Island.

YOUTH

I WANT TO SEE YOU GAVE STRONG;
I WANT TO SEE YOU BE MEN; AND
MANLY; AND I ALSO WANT TO SEE
YOU GENTLE AND TENDER

BE PRACTICAL AS WELL AS
GENEROUS IN YOUR IDEALS. KEEP
YOUR EYES ON THE STARS, BUT
REMEMBER TO KEEP YOUR
FEET ON THE GROUND

ABOVE: *Theodore Roosevelt Island is reached by a footbridge from Virginia.*

LEFT: *A statue of Theodore Roosevelt and plaques are found in the Memorial Plaza.*

12.

The Tidal Basin

T HE TIDAL BASIN is renowned for its Japanese cherry trees and the Jefferson Memorial. It is located southwest of the National Mall and is part of West Potomac Park. Covering over 100 acres and averaging 10 feet deep, it was created in the late 1800s to drain the Washington Channel after high tide and to provide recreational space. The Franklin Delano Roosevelt Memorial and George Mason Memorial are located nearby.

Mrs. Eliza Scidmore, an American journalist and the first female board member of the National Geographic Society, who had just returned from Japan in 1885, came up with the idea of planting cherry trees along the Potomac waterfront. After years of being refused, she appealed in 1909 to a supportive first lady, Helen Taft. It was Dr. Jokichi Takamine, the Japanese chemist

Spring rains overflowing the Tidal Basin lend an ominous atmosphere.

who discovered adrenaline and who happened to be in Washington, DC, at that time, who donated the money for over 3,000 cherry trees. In 1912 the first two cherry trees were planted on the northern bank of the Tidal Basin and south end of 17th Street SW by Mrs. Taft and Viscountess Chinda, wife of the Japanese ambassador; these two trees still exist and are located near the John Paul Jones statue.

Of the approximate 3,750 cherry trees currently surrounding the basin, about 75 percent are Yoshino cherry trees, which have single white blossoms. Other varieties include the Akebono, peaking at the same time but having a pink tint, and the Higan, blooming earlier and having dark pink to white flowers and single or double flowers. East Potomac Park has Kwanzan cherry trees that peak two weeks later than the Yoshino and have thick clusters of pink double blossoms. Bloom times vary, but the annual Cherry Blossom Festival usually runs from the end of March through mid-April, attracting hundreds of thousands of visitors to this rite of spring. Renting a paddle boat at anytime can be a pleasurable endeavor.

The Washington Monument peeks out from behind the cherry blossoms.

ABOVE: *Among a maze of cherry blossoms, a beautiful specimen stands out.*

LEFT: *Cherry blossoms frame the Jefferson Memorial.*

13

Tregaron Estate

T HE 20-ACRE TREGARON ESTATE is nestled between the lovely residential neighborhoods of Cleveland Park and Woodley Park, Washington, DC. Six of the acres and the buildings belong to the Washington International School. The remaining 13 acres belong to the Tregaron Conservancy, a nonprofit organization that is restoring the grounds and has opened them to the public.

The original 40-acre estate, Twin Oaks, was purchased in the 1880s by Gardiner Greene Hubbard, the founder of the National Geographic Society. In 1911, James and Alice Maury Parmele bought a 20-acre piece of the estate. The Parmeles then hired Charles Adams Platt, a leading architect of country houses, and Ellen Biddle Shipman, a well-known landscape

ABOVE: *The foliage is very dense and green in the woodland.*

RIGHT: *Recently exposed, the stone steps add secrecy to the garden.*

architect. Buildings and gardens were designed so that the house and views, to and from it, were integrated with the landscape. This estate, originally named The Causeway, was listed on the National Register of Historic Places in 1989. It is one of Platt and Shipman's most important collaborations, and the only one remaining.

As you walk through the shaded grounds of Tregaron Estate, you will think you have entered a secret garden. Some of the steep stone stairways have recently been unearthed, and the lily pond has been restored and enriched with aquatic plants. Many picturesque stone bridges traverse the winding streams, and the trails and bridle paths cross hilly terrain through beautiful meadows and woodlands.

14.

Tudor Place

L OCATED IN GEORGETOWN a few
blocks away from Dumbarton Oaks
Gardens is Tudor Place, the home
of Martha Washington's granddaughter
Martha Custis Peter, and her husband,
Thomas Peter. The Federal-style house
sits on 5.5 acres, several acres less than
what it had when it was bought in 1805.
The land was used for planting fruit and
vegetables and as grazing land for horses
and cows. It was Armistead Peter III, the
last of six generations of the Peter family
to live there, who completed many of the
garden projects and created the Tudor
Place Foundation. The house and gardens
were opened to the public in 1988.

The northern garden has separate garden rooms, and the eastern part, formerly
a tennis court, now has a lawn with magnolia, crape myrtle, and hydrangea. The
center of the garden, the Flower Knot,
lies within a French parterre. Heirloom

hybrid tea and floribunda roses make the air intoxicating with their fragrance. Perennials, such as peonies and foxglove, contribute to the seasonal array. At the western edge of the garden is the former Bowling Green, where now a lovely lily pond and the Summer House lie at opposite ends of the shaded area. Closest to the house is the English boxwood Ellipse, planted by Martha Peter.

In earlier times, a vista of the Georgetown waterfront could be seen from the southern portico. Now when looking down the open expanse of the sloping lawn, you can marvel at the 100-foot-tall tulip poplar tree with its 15-foot circumference.

BELOW: *The lovely lily pool and statue are at one end of the former Bowling Green.*

RIGHT: *Roses and foxglove thrive in the Flower Knot in the back of the house.*

ABOVE: *The lovely lily pool and statue are at one end of the former Bowling Green.*

LEFT: *Colorful hydrangea adorn the brick walk.*

15.

The United States Botanic Garden

T HE UNITED STATES BOTANIC GARDEN is located on the National Mall at the foot of Capitol Hill and is the country's oldest public garden. It comprises the Victorian-style conservatory, the Bartholdi Park located across Independence Avenue SW from the conservatory, and the National Garden adjacent to the conservatory, with entrances from Independence Avenue SW, Maryland Avenue SW, and the conservatory terrace.

The institution's aim is to demonstrate the aesthetic, economic, therapeutic, cultural, and ecological significance of plants to the well-being of humanity. It accomplishes this by presenting exquisite plant displays, promoting botanical education through educational programs and curated plant collections, and furthering plant conservation by acting as a depository for rare species.

The first botanic garden was created in 1820 on the mall, due to the vision of George Washington, Thomas Jefferson, and James Madison. The garden

Children love to play in the outdoor Children's Garden, watering the plants, playing with water, or digging in the soil. Scarlet beebalm's red flowers attract hummingbirds; its leaves have a minty scent.

lasted only 17 years, but the idea was resurrected in 1850 by Congress, when a large collection of rare plants from around the world collected by the U.S. Exploring Expedition needed care and stewardship. The location of the current conservatory dates to 1933, and the Botanic Garden has been administered through the Office of the Architect of the Capitol since 1934. The Bartholdi Park was named in 1932 and features a large fountain sculpted by Frédéric Auguste Bartholdi, who also created the Statue of Liberty. The National Garden opened in 2006.

The 50,946-square-foot conservatory includes two galleries, two courtyards, and an orangery in addition to the glasshouse with eight garden rooms representing different habitat conditions. In the warmer months, the outdoor terrace features garden exhibits on themes such as pollination, plants for health, food, and spice, or heirloom plants. The Garden Court is the first room, and the permanent collections on display here include economic plants, or those that supply material for food, fiber, beverages, spices, cosmetics, and other uses. One wonderful example is the large cacao tree just inside the entrance on the opposing wall. You will often see large pods, which have many seeds, or cocoa beans, inside. The Garden Court is also the site of the wonderful winter holiday display in which miniature replica Washington landmarks made of plant materials are exhibited alongside beautiful poinsettia displays. For example, the Jefferson Memorial's dome is made from a dried gourd. Throughout the year the Garden Court is enlivened by colorful plants of the season.

The Garden Primeval, on the eastern

Towering palm trees grow in the Jungle, with steps and balustrade in the background.

side, has a terrific collection of ferns. Every plant is labeled, and it is easy and fun to learn the names of some, such as the round leaf fern, fishtail fern, and oil fern. The Hawaii room is next; on the waterfall, look for the interesting cabbage on a stick, a critically endangered plant from Kauai. The World Deserts room has many succulents, and there is an entire room devoted to orchids. In-between is a collection devoted to the display of medicinal plants. The 93-foot domed Jungle represents a tropical rainforest. As you walk down the balustrade and hear and see the pools of water, feel the mist on your face, and see the large logs, vines, and tall palms, such as the large strangler fig, you might think you were in an abandoned tropical plantation. You can even view the forest canopy from the upper walkway.

Different plant displays are seasonally exhibited next to the lovely blue-tiled pool in the formal Garden Court. A bamboo orchid graces the left side and a begonia cultivar is on the right.

The lush foliage and warm moist air of the Jungle is enchanting on a cold, dreary day.

The Bartholdi Park features demonstration gardens and innovative designs that can be incorporated into one's own garden. The 30-foot-high Bartholdi fountain is the centerpiece of the park. It is decorated with fanciful turtles, frogs, fish, cherubs, and three sea nymphs that appear to hold up an overflowing basin. This garden too has numerous miniature gardens. For example, the Rock Garden showcases Hinoki false cypress, and hens and chicks and other small succulents between the rocks. Nearby is a wonderful Summer Chocolate mimosa, with greenish brown leaves and pink, feathery-soft flowers. As you pass the finestem needlegrass, an ornamental feather grass, it is hard to resist touching it to see how soft it is. It is instructive to visit the park many times throughout the warm months, as different flowers take center stage, from irises in the spring to lilies and oleander in June.

The National Garden provides a living laboratory for environmental, botanical, and horticultural education in reflective surroundings. Many varieties of our na-

The popular and hardy peace rose has pink-tinged edges on its yellow petals.

tional flower, the rose, are displayed in the Rose Garden. Roses selected for the garden are those that grow well without chemicals in Washington's hot urban setting. Other garden rooms are the Butterfly Garden and the First Ladies Water Garden, the latter representing the role that water plays in sustaining plant and animal life. The Regional Garden features plants from the larger mid-Atlantic region, selected from the Coastal Plain and Piedmont provinces of states from New Jersey to North Carolina.

The First Ladies Water Garden has a colonial-era quilt pattern design.

The Bartholdi Fountain, lit up at night, imparts a European feel. Nearby, the Conservatory is bathed in blue.

ABOVE: *Narrow and elegant, the Sky Pencil, a type of Japanese holly, provides a lovely vertical accent. Blue irises are in the foreground.*

LEFT: *Tulips border the wall surrounding the Bartholdi Garden.*

ABOVE: *All the classes of roses grown today are represented in the National Garden's Margaret Hagedorn Rose Garden.*

RIGHT: *Irises, cattails, and other water plants and fish can be found in the pond at the far end of the National Garden.*

16.

The United States National Arboretum

T HE UNITED STATES NATIONAL ARBORETUM occupies 446 acres in northeast Washington, DC, and is administered by the Agricultural Research Service of the U.S. Department of Agriculture. In 1927, the U.S. Congress authorized the establishment of the arboretum, but it was not until 1956 that it officially opened. However, people started visiting on weekends in the late 1940s when thousands of newly planted azaleas burst into color. The mission of the arboretum is scientific research, education, display gardens, and conservation.

The National Arboretum is home to many diverse plant collections and has very extensive azalea and rhododendron collections. Frequent visits during the year are needed to absorb the stunning beauty of the plants at their peak and their many splendid fragrances. The labeling of numerous specimens adds to your learning enjoyment.

One of the country's largest bonsai collections is housed within the arboretum's National Bonsai and Penjing Museum, where there are bonsai from China, Japan, and North America. To celebrate the bicentennial, Japan gave the U. S. over 50

The Higo camellia bonsai, in training since 1876, blooms once a year with vibrant red flowers.

world-class bonsai. One of the bonsai, a Japanese White Pine, is nearly 400 years old and survived the atomic blast of the Hiroshima bomb just 2 miles away. Most of the plants are 1- to 4-feet high and are maintained by the pruning of roots and branches and the pinching of new growth. Stylistic features that add to their aura may include asymmetry, as bonsai are not cen-

tered in the container; the appearance of being windswept; and presentation as a miniature forest, such as several juniper trees in one container. Tropical bonsai such as bougainvillea are housed in a nearby Tropical Conservatory.

Across the road is the National Herb Garden, where every plant is an herb in the four distinct garden rooms: the Knot Garden, with its dwarf versions of evergreens that form geometric patterns; 10 theme gardens that display herbs for cooking, dyes, medicine, fragrance, and industry; the Antique and Heritage Rose Garden; and the Entrance Garden.

You may be pleasantly surprised to see something that seems to be out of ancient Greece in the large meadow opposite the visitor center and Bonsai Museum. These are the National Capitol Columns. The 22 Corinthian columns date from 1828 and were removed from the east portico of the U.S. Capitol during a renovation in 1958. Water streams through a channel to a re-flecting pool below, adding to the majesty of the site.

Look up and across to Mount Hamil-ton, at over 200 feet one of the highest

Acres of azaleas are in bloom in the Morris Azalea Garden.

points in the city. Thousands of hybrid azaleas called the Glenn Dales were planted on the south side. These azaleas were bred to have large flowers, a variety of colors, and the ability to survive Washington's winters. The 40-acre azalea collection is a favorite, and the overlapping bloom times and colors do not disappoint. Walk on one of the many paths to Lee Garden to see the tranquil pond and late-blooming azaleas.

Other noteworthy collections are the Asian Collection, the Fern Valley, the Gotelli Dwarf and Slow-Growing Conifer Collection, the National Boxwood Collection, and the Dogwood Collection. You can bike, hike, or drive on the nearly 10 miles of paved roads.

ABOVE: *In the meadow near the Knot Garden and Capitol Columns are beautiful yoshino cherry trees.*

LEFT: *Many varieties of hybrid cherry trees are in the research nursery.*

17

Washington National Cathedral Gardens

T HE WASHINGTON NATIONAL CATHEDRAL is the sixth largest cathedral in the world, and it sits on the highest spot in Washington, DC. Both the National Cathedral and its gardens were started in 1907. The gardens, also known as the cathedral close, were designed by Frederick Law Olmsted with assistance from Florence Brown Bratenahl, the wife of the second dean of the cathedral. Although the cathedral and its grounds occupy nearly 60 acres, it is the Bishop's Garden that is the focal point of the grounds. A 12th-century Norman arch near the Herb Cottage Gift Shop is the portal to the divine Bishop's Garden.

Walled grounds of medieval Gothic cathedrals in Europe and Great Britain were the basis for the garden's design. The plants and herbs selected for the garden have culinary and medicinal purposes, as did the plants in medieval monastic gardens. To instill a sense of eternity, there are Bible-inspired plantings, native plants, and mature specimens of evergreens. There is also an herb garden, rose garden, perennial borders, and trees and shrubs, such as boxwood, holly, and yew. Stones for the winding walkway came from a quarry belonging to George Washington. Other

ABOVE: *This 18th-century bronze sundial is on a 13th-century capital. The shrub with yellow leaves is a pomegranate, the plant with red flowers is pineapple sage, and the one with purple flowers is Mexican sage.*

LEFT: *The National Cathedral towers over the roses in full bloom in the Bishop's Garden.*

features include a sundial, statuary, and the Shadow House, a gazebo with stone walls.

The garden is a delight for all the senses, from the sounds of the carillon bells to the fragrance of the roses that bloom from May to November. There is a small pond with koi and the benches throughout invite visitors of all ages. Adjacent to the Bishops's Garden is a larger, open, park-like space similar to an English garden. Both of these gardens are among the most peaceful sites in the city, from their close-in views of well-maintained plantings to the view of the awe-inspiring cathedral.

Ladew Topiary Gardens

II. MARYLAND

18.

Adkins Arboretum

T HE ADKINS ARBORETUM is a 400-acre arboretum located within the 4,000-acre Tuckahoe State Park in Ridgely, Maryland, on the Eastern Shore. It is the only public garden to highlight native plants of the mid-Atlantic coastal plain. Originally established in 1972 to be the Maryland state arboretum, it opened in 1980 with a gift from its first patron, Leon Andrus. It was named in honor of the Adkins family of the Eastern Shore, who were friends of Andrus and ardent conservationists.

As you walk across the bridge from the parking lot to the visitor's center, you will be tempted to pause and survey the wonderful 1-acre wetland below for turtles and other creatures. Four miles of paths then wind through gardens, meadows, and woodlands, composed of mature

Squash and other vegetables thrive in the Children's Funshine Garden. The greenhouse and native plant nursery growing containers are in the background.

upland and bottomland hardwood forests. Wildflowers are abundant from late winter to summer, and in autumn the woods are full of fruit of the paw paw trees. Over 600 species of native trees, shrubs, grasses, and wildflowers make a home in the habitat adjoining Tuckahoe Creek.

The meadows attract many animals and birds.

19

Antietam National Battlefield

A NTIETAM NATIONAL BATTLEFIELD occupies 3,250 acres of farmland, pastures, and forests in Sharpsburg, Maryland. It was the first major Civil War combat to occur on Northern soil; 23,000 soldiers were dead or missing after 12 hours of fighting on September 17, 1862, making it the bloodiest one-day battle in American history. The failure of the Confederate Army of Northern Virginia's first invasion into the North gave President Lincoln the confidence to issue the Emancipation Proclamation. Established in 1890 by Congress, the cemetery and battlefield were transferred to the National Park Service in 1933.

Antietam is one of the best preserved Civil War battlefields; it includes 96 monuments, over 500 cannons, and historic snake, worm, or zigzag and five-rail vertical fencing. Burnside Bridge, one of the most historic and recognizable attractions, is located near Snavely Woods, the largest forest and natural area at the site. Impressive views of the battlefield and scenic countryside are afforded by the Observation Tower, located along Sunken Road, or Bloody Lane.

As you walk along the Sunken Road, or Bloody Lane, with zigzag fencing on either side, and reflect on the serenity of the battlefield grounds, a great calm overtakes you. The Mumma and Roulette farmsteads, which existed during the war, are in the distant fields, with somber mountains gazing on. Monuments are suitably placed along the Sunken Road and throughout the battlefield. The bucolic setting, with cornfields, pastures with grazing cows, and wildflower-filled meadows, is so intertwined with the historical monuments that one can easily step back in time to reflect on these hallowed grounds. Environmental and historical restoration projects involving the planting of seedlings and wildflowers are ongoing.

The sight of the cannon belies the bucolic view from the Visitor Center.

The meadow is near the Final Attack Trail, where Union soldiers drove Confederate soldiers out of Maryland in the last 2 1/2 hours of the 12-hour battle that was the bloodiest day of war in American history.

Burnside Bridge is one of the most photographed Civil War-era bridges.

A meadow of foxtails surrounds Roulette Farm.

20

Audubon Naturalist Sanctuary

A UDUBON NATURALIST SANCTUARY is the headquarters of the Audubon Naturalist Society of the Central Atlantic States. The 40-acre property in Chevy Chase, Maryland, houses the non-profit environmental organization whose mission is to instill in the public the importance of preserving the natural resources in the Washington, DC, area.

An American naval officer and his Australian wife, Captain and Mrs. Chester Wells, bought 80 acres and commissioned John Russell Pope, a prominent architect, to design the property's Georgian Revival mansion in the 1920s. The mansion, now listed on the National Register of Historic Places, was given to the Audubon Naturalist Society in 1968. The site of the former

ABOVE: *A path goes through the lovely wildflower meadow; the mansion is in the background.*

LEFT: *Trees frame and provide privacy to the lawn of a former tennis court, now used for wedding ceremonies.*

tennis court is a popular venue for wedding ceremonies, with privacy and serenity afforded by the bordering eastern hemlocks.

A trail less than 1 mile long runs nearly along the perimeter; it is the perfect length for families to explore the abundant wildlife, especially if they look closely. The dormant streambed, with its many dead trees strewn across it, makes a wonderful home for insects and birds. Two wildflower meadows branching down from the house allow deer and other wildlife to rest, while salamanders lie under the rocks and turtles hide under the murky pond waters. The Blair Native Plant Garden focuses on native plants of the Chesapeake Bay Watershed.

21

Brookside Gardens

B ROOKSIDE GARDENS is a 54-acre public garden located within Wheaton Regional Park in Wheaton, Maryland. It opened in 1969, after four years of planning and construction by the Maryland-National Capital Park and Planning Commission. Brookside's mission is to showcase plants that are readily available to the home gardener.

It's likely you will find something new with every visit to Brookside. The gardens are ever changing, and not just because of seasonal blooms, there are many different garden rooms, and the gardeners often experiment with new plants and designs, especially in the Trial Garden. Even in winter, you will be greatly rewarded by seeing lush tropical foliage such as banana trees and bird of paradise plants in one of the two conservatories. The stream and

All families enjoy a stroll near the pond.

bridge are always enchanting, and during the holidays the model train display and poinsettias enhance the magical setting. In summer, the conservatory is home to hundreds of butterflies during the Wings of Fancy exhibit.

Another breathtaking sight is the Japanese Tea House overlooking the large pond and Gude Garden, a Japanese-style landscape. You can sit inside and watch the turtles in the water, with the peaceful rolling lawn in the background. Fragrant viburnum beckons you to linger in the gazebo by the other pond.

The several hundred different types of azaleas and rhododendrons offer a magnificent extended bloom, often lasting through the late spring. The adjoining Children's Garden has whimsical structures composed of natural materials, such as cones and twigs. Children can climb in the tree house made from re-purposed materials.

The formal gardens include the Perennial Garden, with its pool and tropical water lilies and wisteria; the Fragrance Garden, consisting of fragrant flowers and plants, with an herb hill that includes medicinal, edible, and fragrant plants and herbs such as mint, basil, fennel, and celery; the Yew Garden, with its annuals; and the Maple Terrace. Nearby is the Rose Garden, with its abundant variety, including floribundas and hybrid teas.

The Trial Garden is a riot of color in spring with its many flowering bulbs. Later, it is transformed into a theme garden, such as a companion or food garden. Companion gardening is a method whereby different types of plants are placed in close proximity to each other for mutual benefit, such as planting tomatoes and basil because basil helps tomatoes overcome disease and insects. Useful gardening information is dispensed here, in keeping with Brookside's mission of enriching each visitor's love of gardening.

Gude Garden Tea House overlooks one of the ponds.

ABOVE: *Tulips are overflowing at the garden.*

LEFT: *The banded orange butterfly is native to Mexico.*

Spring is a wonderful time to see the azaleas and daffodils in bloom near the pond.

The wisteria arbor in the nearby Rose Garden provides a perfect backdrop for the pansies and hyacinth foliage in the Trial Garden.

22

Chesapeake & Ohio Canal National Historic Park

GREAT FALLS

THE CHESAPEAKE & OHIO CANAL NATIONAL Historic Park comprises over 19,000 acres for a distance of 184 miles, from Washington, DC, to Cumberland, Maryland. The goal of the C&O Canal, to link the Chesapeake Bay with the Ohio River headwaters in Pittsburgh, was one of George Washington's visions. Historical features along the canal include lockhouses, pump houses, aqueducts, and dams. One of the most spectacular natural attractions in the region, Great Falls, is accessed from the park near the Great Falls Tavern Visitor Center in Potomac, Maryland (it can also be viewed from Great Falls Park in McLean, Virginia).

Great Falls consists of a series of cascades and rapids that drop nearly 80 feet in just a ⅔-mile stretch of the Potomac River, making it the most vertical and dramatic fall line rapids of any Eastern river. The river

ABOVE: *The Virginia side of Great Falls offers a different but equally incredible view.*

RIGHT: *There are excellent views from the towpath that don't require strenuous hiking.*

is slow-moving just above and below the falls, but as the river narrows from almost 1,000 feet to between 60 and 100 feet at Mather Gorge, the rushing whitewater never fails to excite. As you approach the overlook, you can hear the raging torrent of water as it gushes through sharp crevices.

One can almost feel the spray of the water and the adrenaline rush of the kayakers.

The Charles F. Mercer *is a canal boat pulled by mules that starts at the* Great Falls Visitor Center *in Maryland.*

Many holes filled with rainwater are found on the trail.

BILLY GOAT TRAIL

THE BILLY GOAT TRAIL is located within the Chesapeake & Ohio Canal National Historic Park, on Bear Island between the Potomac River and the part of the canal known as Widewater. There are three sections of the trail, but the most famous is the "A" sec-tion, described below. It can be accessed from the towpath just below the Great Falls overlook or the Old Angler's Inn.

Although the hike begins in Maryland several miles from the DC border, the trail leads you through rugged wilderness. The 1.7-mile trail involves arduous rock scram-bling, hence the trail's name, providing beautiful and spectacular views of the Potomac River and Mather Gorge. The trail goes through woodland and over large boulders, passes sandy beaches and numerous rock pools and ponds, and involves scaling a steep cliff face called the Spitzbergen Cliffs.

In addition to breathtaking views of the Potomac, you may also see a colorful group of kayakers or paddle borders far below, great blue herons soaring overhead in the gorge, or rock climbers rappelling on Virginia shore's steep rocky face.

The blue trail marker and the boulders indicate the Billy Goat Trail and the need for rock scrambling.

23

Ladew Topiary Gardens

LADEW TOPIARY GARDENS are located in Monkton, Maryland, in the hunt country-side of Harford County. It is considered one of the great topiary gardens of the world; the Garden Club of America called it "the most outstanding topiary garden in America."

Harvey S. Ladew grew up in Long Island, New York, and was lured to Maryland by his love of foxhunting. He fell in love with the countryside and in 1929 purchased the more than 200-acre property known as Pleasant Valley Farm. He traveled extensively to England, where he came across the art of topiary in the form of a clipped hunt scene above a hedge. He also became enamored with English and Italian land-scape design, which included the concept of "garden rooms" and long vistas. With some help from the local farmers, he transformed 22 acres of the property formerly used for crops and livestock. Ladew grew, trained, and maintained the topiary shapes himself and thus was awarded the Distinguished Service Medal of the Garden Club of America. The manor house is a 1747 farmhouse that he expanded; be sure to take a tour to learn more of his whimsical personality and the times in which he lived. The house and gardens opened to the public in 1971 and are administered by Ladew Topiary Gardens, Inc., a nonprofit organization whose mission is to maintain and promote the facilities in accordance with Harvey S. Ladew's ingenious spirit.

As you enter the gardens, you will immediately see the stunning topiary of the fox-hunting scene; the horse and rider, hounds, and fox are all made of clipped yew. Further on, there are about 15 different garden rooms, each displaying a unique theme, color, or plant. The Pink Garden showcases only pink blooms, such as pink roses, peonies, and irises. The Rose Garden has many varieties, with climbers displayed beautifully on archways and hybrid tea roses planted in concentric circular beds. The long Yellow Garden has a stream running down the center with yellow irises and goldfish and tadpoles

The statue of Adam and Eve in the Garden of Eden is adorned with blooming azaleas in springtime.

within. The Sculpture Garden displays whimsical topiary designs, such as sea horses, a victory sign, a chalice, and lyre-birds. The Great Bowl has large expanses of lawn and is used for concerts. Nearby, topiary swans still swim on wave-shaped yews. The Terrace Garden near the house has many more topiaries shaped from hemlock, including obelisks, swags, and window openings. Many statuary and whimsical structures are found throughout the property, such as the Tivoli Tea House and Garden, its façade formerly the ticket booth for London's Tivoli Gardens.

The formal Rose Garden is enclosed by brick walls on which there are
espaliered apple and pear trees.

ABOVE: *Yellow irises take center stage in the Yellow Garden's stream, while golden privet hedges follow on the sides.*

RIGHT: *The Water Lily Garden is home to frogs and provides a pleasant place to rest.*

ABOVE: *A whimsical yellow birdhouse and straw bee skeps are found in the Yellow Garden.*

LEFT: *Mr. Ladew's love of water garden features, seen here near the Terrace Garden, was influenced by his many visits to gardens overseas.*

24

McCrillis Gardens

McCRILLIS GARDENS in Bethesda, Maryland, is a 5-acre shade garden managed by Brookside Gardens. Its former owners, William and Virginia McCrillis, donated the garden in 1978 to the Maryland-National Capital Park and Planning Commission. William McCrillis was a special assistant to the Secretary of the Interior under several presidential administrations. The house is used as a gallery to exhibit the work of local artists.

The garden is best known for its extensive azalea collection, whose peak viewing time is early April to early June. Rhododendrons are also plentiful, and other tree specimens, ferns, grasses, perennials, and annuals add color and texture throughout the year. Meandering paths, several lawns, a gazebo, and a plethora of benches throughout add to the enjoyment of this shade garden.

ABOVE: *The Brookside Gardens School of Botanical Art and Illustration is located on the first floor of the McCrillis house.*

RIGHT: *The azaleas look like peppermint candy.*

25.

McKee-Beshers Wildlife Management Area

THE MCKEE-BESHERS WILDLIFE MANAGEMENT AREA occupies 2,000 acres of woodlands, fields, swamps, creeks, and wooded bottomland in Poolesville, Maryland. There are several access points and parking lots off River Road or Hunting Quarters Road. The land is managed by the Wildlife and Heritage Service of the Maryland Department of Natural Resources. Its mission is to enhance wildlife populations and their respective habitats and to provide public recreational use of the state's wildlife resources.

On the many miles of trails, you may see deer, wild turkey, waterfowl, amphibians, and reptiles. Water lilies are abundant in the wetlands, and you will often see great blue herons or great egrets on the water's distant edge. Every year, a tract of several acres is planted with sunflowers to attract wildlife for hunters, but in July that area is a major attraction for nature photographers and tourists.

Queen Anne's Lace lives up to its name.

The wetlands at McKee-Beshers lie in a floodplain of the Potomac River and are a good place for wildlife and bird-watching.

Green Spring Gardens

III. VIRGINIA

26.
George Washington's Mount Vernon Estate, Museum & Gardens

MOUNT VERNON, the most visited historic estate in the United States, is located in Mount Vernon, Virginia, just 16 miles south of Washington, DC. At the time of his death, George Washington owned 8,000 acres divided into five separate farms. Mansion House Farm is where Washington lived with his family, and Mount Vernon, at 500 acres, is part of that property.

George Washington's great grandfather, John Washington, acquired the estate in 1674, and when the widow of George Washington's half-brother died in 1761, the land passed on to George Washington. He lived there with his wife, Martha, until his death in 1799. Not only did Washington increase the size of the farmhouse and design and build all 12 outbuildings, he also designed the grounds to reflect his life as a country gentleman. The rolling meadows, pleasure and kitchen gardens, winding pathways, and groves of trees were all designed by Washington.

In 1858 the Mount Vernon Ladies' Association purchased

Mount Vernon from the Washington family, and two years later the estate was opened to the public. Mount Vernon is a wonderful place to visit for both its historical buildings and grounds. The mansion and twelve buildings are original (there are four more buildings that are reconstructed), and you can reflect on George Washington's exceptional garden designs or be captivated by wonderful views of the Potomac River.

George Washington was the nation's first president, a distinguished military leader, and statesman, but he was also a great farmer. He tested out many field crops. In the small Botanical Garden there are examples of exotic plants with which he experimented, such as southern magnolia trees. Friends from overseas and from far away in the United States sent him seeds, and he carefully noted the seeds' progress to determine their feasibility.

The wharf is not original but a splendid addition.

The estate's grounds include many specific gardens, beautiful lawns, woods, animal pastures, open acreage, and memorials. The Bowling Green is the impressive large green lawn stretching inland, lined with many old trees, including two tulip poplar trees planted by Washington in 1785. He designed these pleasure grounds and the land beyond to the west gate entrance to create beautiful distant vistas. The house is situated on a high bluff above the Potomac River, affording grand views of the river's bends from the majestic sloping lawn.

Renovation of the Upper Garden to reflect Washington's actual pleasure garden began in 2005 and is now complete. The main changes were that the garden paths were widened and old English boxwoods were removed, making way for many more heirloom flowers, such as larkspur and foxglove, and vegetables, such as peas, pole beans, lettuce, and cabbage. In George Washington's time, the spectacular display of many herbaceous plants surrounding the vegetables served to impress visitors. The two lovely boxwood parterres with a fleur-de-lis pattern, guarded by lovely

A parterre of boxwood in a fleur-de-lis pattern has been re-created. In the background are containers of tropical plants, similar to those that George Washington would have grown in his greenhouse.

Mount Vernon and its expansive lawn are superbly sited above the Potomac River.

tropical plants, including hibiscus and lime and grapefruit trees, add to the garden's glory. Espaliered cherry trees adorn the brick walls.

The Kitchen Garden, or Lower Garden, is on the other side of the Bowling Green. Enclosed by lovely brick walls that provide warmth to the many espaliered apple trees, the many vegetables grown within include squash, cabbage, and lettuce. Many cordons of pear and apple trees define the brick pathways of the garden and add to its charm.

The Fruit Garden and Nursery, located below the paddock, is an orchard containing plum, peach, and apple trees. Other vegetables including squash, potatoes, and lettuce are also cultivated. The Pioneer Farm site is located at the bottom of the estate, near the wharf. Its notable feature is a reproduction of Washington's invention, a 16-sided treading barn to process wheat and other grains.

Washington's tomb is located along a peaceful tree-lined pathway with a cedar of Lebanon tree planted during the centennial celebration of Washington's death. Further on the path in a wooded setting is the Slave Memorial honoring the slaves that worked at Mount Vernon; it is thought that the hillside holds as many as 75 graves.

George Washington and his guests could enjoy scenic views of the Potomac River from this porch.

A re-creation of George Washington's 16-sided treading barn for processing wheat and other grains is on the Pioneer Farmer site.

Vegetables, including lettuce, beans, and squash, grow in the Lower Garden; the seed storage building is in the background.

27.

Green Spring Gardens

GREEN SPRING GARDENS is a delightful 28-acre oasis of green in Alexandria, Virginia. The intent of the gardens is to display pragmatic landscaping designs that can be used by Washington area residents. There are more than 20 themed demonstration gardens, a woodland trail with ponds, and a greenhouse with tropical plants.

The gardens were originally part of a 540-acre property on which John Moss built a house in 1784. He and successive owners supplanted tobacco with corn, wheat, other crops, and livestock. The last residents were Michael and Belinda Straight, who bought the house and 33 adjoining acres in 1942. They used this country estate to entertain, and they hired Beatrix Farrand to design the garden surrounding it, where she planted roses, boxwood hedges, and perennials. The house and 16 acres were given in 1970 to the Fairfax County Park Authority, which acquired 11 additional acres to establish Green Spring Gardens.

As you enter the gardens, you will notice the parking lot is bordered with many flower gardens, whose plantings change with the seasons. Walking through to the gazebo, you encounter the large lawn framed by the themed gardens surrounding it. Heading counterclockwise to the Horticulture Center, notice the diverse plant varieties in the Rock Garden, including phlox, juniper, and cypress. Three small gardens show possible landscape designs for a townhouse, family, or backyard wildlife habitat garden. The woodland trail with its native plants, two ponds and water lilies may tempt you off the pathway. Be sure to check out the Kitchen Garden for the colorful array and spectacular show of vegetables. Apple and pear trees are in the orchard, alongside stunningly espaliered grape vines. Roses, peonies, sage, and other plants compete for your senses in the showy roses and companions display

A London plane tree near the manor house has beautiful mottled bark on its trunk.

garden closer to the house. As you go through the shaded Garden Walk, notice some unique features of the plants, such as the beautiful cinnamon-colored curly stripped bark of the paperbark maple tree.

These Moroccan poppies are in full bloom.

Blue Nigella, or Love in a Mist, and pink shrub roses are seen
in the Roses and Companions Garden.

*The bunny seems bewildered by the wonderful assortment of vegetables grown here,
including arugula, tomatoes, leeks, and many types of lettuce.*

28.
Huntley Meadows Park

HUNTLEY MEADOWS PARK occupies 1,425 acres in the Hybla Valley section of Alexandria and is the largest park in Fairfax County. Located just off bustling U.S. 1, the park is a hidden gem of young hardwood forests, wildflower-filled meadows, and freshwater wetlands, the latter comprising about 500 acres. Its plant life and wildlife are among the most diverse in the metropolitan area.

The parkland was originally part of a plantation owned by George Mason IV, of Gunston Hall, a 5,500-acre tobacco and corn plantation owned by the Virginia senior statesman. Wheat, corn, and hay were cultivated on the flat land. In 1825 one of his grandsons built a Federal-style home, now called Historic Huntley, on part of the land. It is only open to school and scout groups. Mason family members lived here into the early 1900s. An entrepreneur wanted to build a zeppelin aviation park in the late 1920s.

When that failed, the federal government acquired the land and used it until 1970. In 1975 President Gerald Ford donated the land to Fairfax County, and the park was created with an additional purchase of 165 adjacent wetland acres by the Fairfax County Park Authority.

Upon entering, the visitor walks through a dense forest of young hardwoods before reaching the Visitor Center. The Observation Tower is only about ¾ mile from the Visitor Center, but it may take you awhile since the path is a boardwalk above shallow water, there is no railing, and you may want to peer off both sides of the boardwalk to see the creatures lurking below. It is very easy to find snakes, tadpoles, frogs, and, in the larger body of water beyond, turtles. Lucky visitors may spot a beaver or muskrat. The background sound of the cattails swaying in the slightest breeze is calming, only broken by the melodic sounds of bullfrogs and birds and other rustling sounds in the wetlands. Over 200 species of birds have been observed in the park, and it is one of the best places to view migrating birds in the spring and fall. Beyond the observa-

Beavers are just some of the abundant wildlife at the park.

tion tower the trail continues, making a loop for 1.75 miles. The park has another entrance at the intersection of South Kings Highway and Telegraph Road, from which a 1.2-mile hiking and biking trail leads to a large observation deck.

A hardwood forest surrounds the wetlands.

PARENTS
PLEASE HELP
US KEEP THE
SAND IN THE
SAND BOX

29.

Meadowlark Botanical Gardens

SOME WINDING BUCOLIC ROADS can still be found not far from the bustling commercial center of Tysons Corner in Vienna, Virginia. Off one of these roads, just 5 miles away, are the magnificent Meadowlark Botanical Gardens.

Caroline Ware, a social historian, and Gardiner Means, an economist, moved from New England to work on the New Deal programs of the Franklin Roosevelt administration. They were early environmentalists who bought a 74-acre farm in 1935 and planted flower gardens. They donated their farm to the Northern Virginia Park Authority in 1980. The land was combined with a 21 acre parcel of land nearby and opened as a public garden seven years later. Additions in those early years included three lakes and numerous bridges, gazebos, walking trails, picnic tables.

Shortly after walking through the well-appointed Visitor Center, the path leads you to a breathtaking vista as the land quickly drops off and you see lakes

The Korean Bell Garden is the first one in a public setting in North America. Figures of birds, animals, and plants are featured on the bell.

with fountain sprays, backed by meadows and framed by the distant forest. Gardens of seasonal flowers are abundant on that high point of land. As you walk down the path, you will come to the first of the lakes, Lake Gardiner. It is especially serene as willow trees sway over the shore, water lilies provide shelter for the fish, and cat-tails rustle in the breeze. Lake Gardiner also contains a delightful sand area for

children and an arched wooden bridge reminiscent of Monet's water garden in Giverny. Lake Caroline, the large lake nearby, has a wooden walkway leading to a gazebo, which is a great place to observe the many fish, turtles, and ducks living nearby. The third and smallest, Lake Lina, is home to many frogs and snakes.

The gardens have many collections of plants, including hostas, lilacs, cherry trees, day lilies, native plants, herbs, and woodlands. One special collection of note, the Potomac Valley Native Plant Collection, is an active conservation program with Virginia blue bells, prickly-pear cactus, paw paw, native wildflowers, and many spectacular native species.

Meadowlark Gardens is now the only garden in the country to have a Korean garden with a Korean bell. There is also a historic log cabin from the mid-1700s, and a new addition is the nearby Children's Garden, which demonstrates the usage of plants through time.

The Botanical Gardens also have a woodland trail, rolling meadows, and ruins of a springhouse. Its Atrium is a popular venue for weddings and events.

Cattails frame serene Lake Gardiner. Built between islands in the lake, this picturesque bridge made of seven native hardwoods is both arched and curved.

An expansive lawn is visible beyond Lake Caroline and its gazebo.

Daylilies such as Miss Jessie and Sugar Cookie are in the collection on the path down toward the lakes.

Riverbend Park

R IVERBEND PARK, administered by the Fairfax County Park Authority, occupies over 400 acres along the Potomac River, just up from Great Falls, Virginia. The park has an extensive trail network, boat launch and rentals, nature center, and picnic areas.

Its trail network of approximately 10 miles passes upland forests of beech and sycamore, meadows, and ponds. Paw paw trees border its namesake trail that hugs the Potomac River part of the way. Along the 2.5 mile Potomac Heritage Trail that connects with Great Falls Park there are stunning views of the Potomac River, nearby small islands, and a dam. The pleasurable sound of the rushing water over the dam's small water-falls is a prelude to Great Falls, just another mile further south. The river is very shallow and rocky upstream from the boat launch, offering beautiful views to kayakers and canoeists of is-land rocks with plant life. The park is carpeted with Virginia bluebells and other spring wild-flowers in late March and early April.

ABOVE: *These still waters are bound for a surprise as they near Great Falls!*

RIGHT: *A heron wades and waits for dinner to come by.*

31

River Farm

R IVER FARM, the 25-acre property
that serves as the headquarters of
the American Horticultural Society (AHS), is located between Mount Vernon and Old Town Alexandria. The AHS's
mission is to involve more people, including children, in gardening and to promote
earth-friendly gardening techniques.

River Farm was once part of a much
larger tract of land that George Washington owned, which was the northernmost
of his five farms. The original house on
the property was built in the mid-1700s
and then extensively revamped in the
early 1900s. Enid Annenberg Haupt, a
philanthropist and gardener, provided the
funds that allowed the AHS to purchase
the property in 1973. Today the house is
a popular venue for weddings and other
events because of its elegant ballroom, at-
tractive gardens, and beautiful sweeping
vistas down the lawn to the Potomac River.

Once owned by George Washington, this historic property now serves as the headquarters of the American Horticultural Society.

On entering the property, a circular driveway offers visitors a view of an orchard and azalea garden. Visitors can sit on the porch of the main house, which houses the AHS offices, and admire the lovely 4-acre André Bluemel Meadow with its abundant wildflowers and grasses that provide habitat for a diverse array of wildlife. Walk down through the meadow to get a closer view of the Potomac River. A sunken Ha-Ha wall, modeled after similar walls in England used to keep livestock out of manor gardens, separates the meadow from the more formal garden areas above.

The English boxwood border has shrubs thought to be 100 years old. Near the annual and perennial beds is a chaste tree, an unusual looking tree that has been pruned to produce large sphere-like clusters of foliage at the ends of the main branches. In the next garden be sure to see the 200-year-old Osage orange tree, considered to be the largest one in the country, along with a small pump house that is covered with a green roof composed mainly of drought-resistant sedums. There are many themed gardens within the Children's Garden, and a visitor with children should make time to enjoy a hands-on experience. The Green Garage display offers take-home ideas for earth-friendly gardening, including another green roof.

A stone sculpture of Pan is at the far end of an allée lined with boxwoods, hydrangeas, and roses.

ABOVE: *A view of the 4-acre André Bluemel Meadow shows off its grasses and perennials.*

RIGHT: *The charming pump house has a green roof covered in drought-resistant plants, primarily sedums.*

The chaste tree is pruned using a technique called pollarding *to produce the large, ball-like masses of leaves.*

Purple asters and switchgrass in the André Bluemel Meadow are some of the nearly 100 different species of grasses and herbaceous perennials.

32

Woodlawn

WOODLAWN OCCUPIES 126 acres of hilltop land that was formerly part of George Washington's Mount Vernon estate. George Washington gave his nephew Major Lawrence Lewis and his bride, Eleanor "Nelly" Parke Custis Lewis, granddaughter of Martha Washington, approximately 2,000 acres for their wedding. Dr. William Thornton, the first architect of the U.S. Capitol, designed the Federal-style house between 1800 and 1805. In 1952, after several owners, Woodlawn became the first historic site owned by The National Trust for Historic Preservation. The Pope-Leighey House designed by Frank Lloyd Wright is also located on the grounds.

A brick pathway leads from the parking area all the way to the distant vegetable garden bordering the woodland. Along the way, the path first passes a lovely lawn that was most likely a bowling green.

ABOVE: *A crape myrtle is in the center of the French parterre of the Formal Garden.*

RIGHT: *The brick walkway extends from the parking area to the large Vegetable Garden, passing an old pignut hickory tree.*

Next are the Formal Gardens consisting of two parterres with old-fashioned heritage roses and borders of English boxwood. They were part of a larger garden designed by renowned landscape designer Alden Hopkins and planted in 1953 during the garden's restoration by the Garden Club of Virginia. At the far end is a large Vegetable Garden planted by Arcadia in 2011. Several nature trails traverse the many acres of fields and woodland.

The Arcadia Center for Sustainable Food & Agriculture is located at Woodlawn. As a nonprofit organization cooperating with the National Trust for Historic Preservation, Arcadia provides experiential learning to schools and community groups and distributes fresh, locally grown food to the metropolitan area.

The gazebo is visible at the end of the large Vegetable Garden planted by
the Arcadia Center for Sustainable Food & Agriculture.

Large Texas lilac bushes are seen near the Colonial Revival–style parterre of the Formal Garden.

Site Information

I. DISTRICT OF COLUMBIA

Dumbarton Oaks
1703 32nd Street, NW (garden entrance
is at R and 31st streets, NW)
Washington, DC 20007
(202) 339-6450
www.doaks.org/gardens/
Regular hours: March 15–Oct 31, Tues–Sun
2 PM–6 PM, $
Winter hours: Nov 1–March 14, Tues–Sun
2 PM–5 PM, free

Dumbarton Oaks Park
Lovers Lane near R Street and 31st Street, NW
Washington, DC 20007
Free

Hillwood Estate, Museum & Gardens
4155 Linnean Avenue, NW
Washington, DC 20008
(202) 686-5807; 1-877-HILLWOOD
www.hillwoodmuseum.org
Open Tues–Sat, 9:30 AM–5 PM, select Sundays; $

Kenilworth Aquatic Gardens
1550 Anacostia Avenue, NE
Washington, DC 20019-2028
(202) 426-6905
www.nps.gov/keaq
Open daily 7AM–4PM, except major holidays; free

Meridian Hill Park
1550 W St. NW
Washington, DC 20009
(202) 661-7581
www.nps.gov/mehi/index.htm
Open daily, daylight hours; free

Montrose Park
3099 R St. NW
Washington, DC 20007
(202) 282-1063
www.montrosepark.org/
Open daily until dark; free

National Gallery of Art Sculpture Garden
700 Constitution Ave. NW
Washington, DC 20565
(202) 289-3310
www.nga.gov/feature/sculpturegarden/general
/index.shtm
Summer hours (Memorial Day-Labor Day),
Mon–Thurs and Sat 10 AM–7 PM, Fri 10 AM–9 PM,
Sun 11 AM–7 PM; other seasonal hours; free

Rock Creek Park
(for Nature Center and Planetarium)
5200 Glover Rd NW
Washington, DC 20015
(202) 895-6070
www.nps.gov/rocr/index.htm

Hours (for Nature Center and Planetarium):
Wed–Sun, 9 AM–5 PM except major holidays; free
Hours, locations, and fees for other park
amenities vary

Smithsonian Gardens
Various locations (see text for location)
and hours vary by season; free
(202) 633-2220
www.gardens.si.edu

Theodore Roosevelt Island
c/o Turkey Run Park
George Washington Memorial Parkway
McLean, VA 22101
(703) 289-2500 (headquarters)
www.nps.gov/this/index.htm
Open daily 6 AM–10 PM; free

The Tidal Basin
Part of West Potomac Park; west of 17th Street SW
and south of Constitution Avenue NW, Washington,
DC 20242
(202) 426-6841
www.npca.org/parks/west-potomac-park.html
Open year round; free

Tregaron Estate
3100 Macomb St. NW
Washington, DC 20008
http://tregaronconservancy.org/about.html
Open daylight hours; free

Tudor Place
1644 31st St. NW
Washington, DC 20007
(202) 965-0400

www.tudorplace.org
Open Tues–Sat, 10 AM–4 PM; $

The United States Botanic Garden
100 Maryland Ave. SW
Washington, DC 20001
(202) 225-8333
www.usbg.gov/
Conservatory hours, 10 AM–5 PM daily; National
Garden summer hours, 10 AM–7 PM; Bartholdi Park,
dawn to dusk; free

The United States National Arboretum
3501 New York Ave. NE
Washington, DC 20002
(202) 245-2726
www.usna.usda.gov
Open daily 8 AM–5 PM; closed Dec. 25; free

Washington National Cathedral Garden
3101 Wisconsin Ave., NW
Washington, DC 20016
(202) 537-6200
www.nationalcathedral.org/visit/moreGardens.shtml
Hours vary; free

II. MARYLAND

Adkins Arboretum
12610 Eveland Rd.
Ridgely, MD 21660
(410) 634-2847
www.adkinsarboretum.org
Open daily, 10 AM–4 PM (except major holidays); $

Antietam National Battlefield
5831 Dunker Church Road (Visitor Center)
Sharpsburg, MD 21782

(301) 432-5124
www.nps.gov/anti/index.htm
Hours for Visitor Center vary by season; Memorial
Day–Labor Day 8:30 AM–6 PM; Labor Day–
Memorial Day 8:30 AM–5 PM; $

Audubon Naturalist Sanctuary

8940 Jones Mill Rd.
Chevy Chase, MD 20815
(301) 652-9188
www.audubonnaturalist.org
Open daily, dawn to dusk; free

Brookside Gardens

1800 Glenallan Ave.
Wheaton, MD 20902
(301) 962-1400
www.montgomeryparks.org/brookside
Open daily sunrise to sunset, except Dec. 25;
Visitor Center 9 AM–5 PM; free

Chesapeake & Ohio Canal National Historic Park

Great Falls Tavern Visitor Center
11710 MacArthur Blvd.
Potomac, MD 20854
(301) 767-3714
www.nps.gov/choh/index.htm
Open daylight hours; parking fee

Ladew Topiary Gardens

3535 Jarrettsville Pike
Monkton, MD 21111
(410) 557-9570
www.ladewgardens.com
Open March 26–Oct 31, Mon–Fri 10 AM–4 PM,
Sat–Sun 10:30 AM–5 PM; $

McCrillis Gardens

6910 Greentree Rd.
Bethesda, MD 20817
(301) 962-14553
www.montgomeryparks.org/brookside/mcrillis
_gardens.shtm
Open daily, 10 AM–sunset; free

McKee-Beshers Wildlife Management Area

16778 River Rd. (just before Hunting Quarter Rd.)
Poolesville, MD 20837
(410) 260-8540
Open daily sunrise to sunset; free

III. VIRGINIA

George Washington's Mount Vernon Estate, Museum & Gardens

3200 Mount Vernon Memorial Highway
Mount Vernon, VA 22309
(703) 780-2000
www.mountvernon.org/
Open year-round; times vary by season; $

Green Spring Gardens

4603 Green Springs Rd.
Alexandria, VA 22312
www.fairfaxcounty.gov/parks/gsgp
Open Mon–Sat. 9 AM–4:30 PM; Sun Noon–4:30 PM;
free

Huntley Meadows Park

3701 Lockheed Blvd.
Alexandria, VA 22306
(703) 768-2525
www.fairfaxcounty.gov/parks/huntley/
Open dawn to dusk; free

Meadowlark Botanical Gardens
9750 Meadowlark Gardens Court
Vienna, VA 22182
(703) 255-3631
www.nvrpa.org/park/meadowlark_botanical
_gardens
Hours vary monthly, 10 AM–5 PM and later in
warmer months; $

Riverbend Park
8700 Potomac Hills Street
Great Falls, VA 22066
(703) 759-9018
www.fairfaxcounty.gov/parks/riverbend
Hours: park grounds 7 AM–dusk; Visitor
Center normal weekdays 9 AM–5 PM, weekends
Noon–5 PM; free

River Farm
7931 East Boulevard Dr.
Alexandria, VA 22308
(703) 768-5700
www.ahs.org/river_farm/index.htm
Open weekdays 9 AM–5 PM, excluding national
holidays; Sat 9 AM–1 PM early April–late Sept.; free

Woodlawn
9000 Richmond Highway
Alexandria, VA 22309
(703) 780-4000
www.woodlawn1805.org
Open Thurs–Mon, 10 AM–5 PM; $

Bibliography

Adkins Arboretum, http://adkinsarboretum.org

Antietam National Battlefield, www.nps.gov/anti/index.htm

Audubon Naturalist Society, www.audubonnaturalist.org

Billy Goat Trail, www.nps.gov/choh/planyourvisit/upload/greatfallstrail descriptions.pdf

Brookside Gardens, MontgomeryParks.org, www.montgomeryparks .org/brookside

Chesapeake & Ohio Canal National Historic Park, www.nps.gov/choh/index.htm

DC's Field to Fork Network, www.fieldtoforknetwork.org

Dumbarton Oaks Research Library and Collection, www.doaks.org/gardens/

Dumbarton Oaks Park, www.tclf.org/landscapes/dumbarton-oaks-park

Green Spring Gardens, www.fairfaxcounty.gov/parks/gsgp

Hillwood Estate, Museum & Gardens, www.hillwoodmuseum.org

Huntley Meadows Park, www.fairfaxcounty.gov/parks/huntley/

Kenilworth Aquatic Gardens, www.nps.gov/nr/travel/wash/dc95.htm

Ladew Topiary Gardens, www.ladewgardens.com

McCrillis Gardens, www.montgomeryparks.org/brookside

McKee-Beshers Wildlife Management Area, www.dnr.state.md.us/wildlife /publiclands/central/mckeebeshers.asp

Meadowlark Botanical Gardens, www.bgci.org/garden.php?id＝3458&ftr Country＝&ftrKeyword＝Meadowlark＋Gardens&ftrl

Montrose Park, www.tclf.org/landscapes/montrose-park

Meridian Hill Park, http://nps.gov/mehi/historyculture/index.htm

Mount Vernon, www.mountvernon.org/

National Gallery of Art Sculpture Garden, www.nga.gov/exhibitions/sculpture
info/shtm

Riverbend Park, www.fairfaxcounty.gov/parks/riverbend/

River Farm, www.ahs.org/river-farm/index.htm

Rock Creek Park, www.npt.gov/rocr/index.htm

Smithsonian Gardens, www.gardens.si.edu/horticulture/gardens1.htm

Theodore Roosevelt Island, www.nps.gov/history/history/online_books/presidents
/site11.htm

The Tidal Basin, www.nps.gov/cherry/cherry-blossom-history.htm

Tregaron Estate, http://tregaronconservancy.org/

Tudor Place, www.tudorplace.org

United States Botanic Garden, www.usbg.gov/index.cfm

The United States National Arboretum, www.usna.usda.gov/

Washington National Cathedral, www.nationalcathedral.org/visit/moreGardens.shtml

Woodlawn, www.woodlawn1805.org